A Father's Faith

*A collection of prayers given
to the Young Men's Bible Class,
The First Presbyterian Church
of Greensboro, North Carolina*

*by
John F. Davis*

A Father's Faith
by John F. Davis

With introduction and illustrations
by Molly Davis

Printed in the United States of America.

First printing edition 2019.

Published by Preserving the Vision
5635 Quarry Court
Boulder, Colorado, 80301

preservingthevision.org
preservingthevision@gmail.com

ISBN: 978-1-7326491-1-8

Introduction: My Father
by Molly Davis

My father was a simple man as you will see in the pages of the way he thought about life. This book reveals what was important to him: faith, family, friends and fellowship, and of course the sacred tennis ball. I made this book for him and he cherished it. He began writing prayers his for his church fellowship group. He had the worst handwriting I had ever seen, yet, he carefully printed the ones in the back of the book with love in each painful controlled stroke, just to defy his reputation of "handwriting looking like a doctor's chicken scratch."

The book was a mutual labor of love with my father's writing and my illustrations. It is always a bittersweet moment when I read the book. I miss my father very much as well as the illustrative paintings which were lost in the 2013 Boulder flood.

In his eulogy, he would not let me mention his accomplishments and instead said, "I want the First Presbyterian Church to be full of praise with the sound of hymns of the Lord's prayer and my old southern hymns that I love so much like *Rock of Ages.*" He made me promise to do that. I carried out his wishes at the end as he wanted because we had such a mutual respect for each other. He was my best friend, and it was so hard to think that I would not see him again.

He could never carry a tune so he hummed while the songs went. He rubbed my fingers as my hands always hurt in church when it was cold. A huge stained glass windows warmed up the center of the church, but not where we sat. The First Presbyterian Church in Greensboro is a big church. There were a lot of people in that congregation who had money. "Mooney Davis" had been a very poor boy growing up and his home was in the poorest part of Greensboro.

Dad's richness in spirit overflowed with the love that he showed for every man he met—whether it was someone he met along the street in a wheelchair and gave a ride home after stopping off at the grocery store for them, or the black gardener who would come to the door and put his head down to ask for money. At the First Presbyterian Church, he led the young men's bible class which was something of a misnomer with no one under 55. They put their faith in my father to joyously lead them in prayer with a few good jokes as well.

On Saturday night when I was living in Colorado, my father would call and say, "I need a joke also for the class…do you have anything?" At first when he did that I would give a choice of three, one super clean which he said was "too corny," one which was a little off-color and one which was considered locker room humor. Then dad would pick one and I never knew which one he would pick. But when he picked the off-color ones, he would say, "That will do, it is just dirty enough to be funny and clean enough to tell in a young men's bible class." No doubt, if it got a bunch of laughs it was retold at Kiwanis club on Thursdays as well.

When my father died, I kept this book by my side constantly as I missed him so much I thought my heart would break. When dad died, my mother took up residency in an Alzheimer's facility. Since then, I have faced many challenges, and there were the times I wanted to call my father to ask him why bad things happen to good people. Where was he when I needed him most? And all along he was right there walking with me in his ageless echo of faith.

Whether you are a spiritual person or not, take his words to help you in times when things are tough. May his little book inspire and comfort you, as it has for me these 18 years since his passing.

Merry Christmas….2018, Molly Davis

To Dad from Molly Christmas '90

When we are born we are given a
spiritual earthly Father, and a
heavenly father.
I was fortunate to know both.

The Prayers

Milton wrote, "The mind is its own place, and in itself can make Heaven of hell, a Hell of heaven."

Our Father we pray for peace of mind so that we can be effective in achieving peace in the world.

Amen

George Santayana wrote, "There is no cure for birth and death—save to enjoy the interval!"

Our Father we thank you for the gift of life and the promise of life eternal in the meantime may our lives be a living testimony to our gratitude!

Amen

Longfellow wrote, "If we could read the secret history of our enemies we should fine in each man's life—sorrow and suffering and suffering enough to disarm all hostility."

Our Father help us to know hostility is futility—may we strive to *address* the deep needs of our fellow man and *dare* to make friends with our enemies.

Amen

Do all the good you can—by all the means
you can—in all the ways you can—in all
the places you can—at all the times
you can—to all the people you can—as
long as ever you can.

Amen

The fruit of the spirit is love, joy,
peace, patience, kindness, goodness, faithfulness.

Our Father help us to be open to receive your
gift of this fruit—let *love* be our goal and *world
peace* our prayer

Amen

As the body without the spirit is dead—so faith without works is dead *also*.

Our Father help us to respect out body—*enlighten* our spirit *affirm* our faith—and *expand* our works.

Amen

Do all the good you *can*—by all the means you
can—at all the time you can—to all the people
you *can*—as long as ever you *can*.

Amen

Leaf study

K. Gough '90

In everything by prayer and supplication, with *thanksgiving*, let your requests be made known unto God!

Our Father help us to be faithful in prayer—secure in the knowledge that you do *hear* and you do *care*.

Amen

May the words of our *mouth*
and the meditations of our heart be acceptable
in the sight Oh Lord!

Our Father please strength us
in these endeavors.

Amen

"Today is the day the Lord has made—let us rejoice and be happy in it."

Our Father we thank you for the *splendid* gift of each day!

Help us to make each today better than *yesterday*—and each *tomorrow* better than today.

Amen

And now abideth faith, hope, love—these three, but the greatest of these is love.

Our Father we pray our lives will be a living testimony of your love for us and our love for others.

Amen

Our Father help us to make time to reflect on your gifts of life, love, joy, health, family and friends.

Guide us to use your gift of *time*—to nurture these things of true value and meaning.

Amen

Our Father help us to live life fully—with all of its joy and sadness, success and failure, beauty and blight.

Accepting, through faith that you are in charge—we will as your children, arrive at the ultimate goal victoriously!

Amen

Our Father we pray for the small areas of our lives where we live hour by hour.

We touch the lives of so many people and our influence can be so great.

With your help we can make each hour special—help us to help others.

Amen

Our Father we pray for sensitive natures
so we can recognize and nourish those in need;
help us to be more prone to praise,
than to criticize. We are all fragile and need
encouragement. We are all in this life together.
To live it victoriously we need each other
and most of all we need you.

Amen

Our Father, you know us better than we know ourselves—help us to make the self you know acceptable to you.

Amen

Our Father please hear our prayer—help us to live each day so that we do not have to apologize to you or to man for our activities during that small slice of life. Yesterday is gone—tomorrow is not a reality—today is the life we have.

Amen

Our Father we know it is impossible to justify ourselves to you—we know it is impossible to find you through our own efforts—help us to know your grace is sufficient for us.

Help us to know you have already found us—help us to accept the gift of you love and pass it on to others each day.

Amen

Today is the day the Lord has made—let us rejoice and be happy in it.

Our Father help us to be able to rejoice even in the face of trials and tribulations—knowing full well we will ultimately be victorious through faith in you.

Amen

Our Father on this day so special to Christmas throughout the world—help us to know this splendid happening is God's gift of love and grace to us.

All we are called to do is accept this gift graciously, and a life filled with love and meaning will be ours.

Amen

Our Father help us to treasure time as one
of your most precious gifts. At the end
of each day let us reflect on how our time
could have been better lived.

Help us to make each today better than
yesterday and each tomorrow better than today.

Amen

Our Father help us to remember that when we...

     sow a thought we reap an act
     sow an act we reap a habit
     sow a habit we reap a character
     sow a character we reap a destiny

May we sow purity so what we reap will be splendid in your eyes.

Our Father we thank you
for the many blessings you give to us each day.

May our lives be as a revolving door,
so the blessings we receive will flow out
into a needy world.

Amen

Our Father we thank you for this class and for the message brought to us this day.

We pray you will inspire us to a life of service. We pray for good health that we may use our energy to help others; we pray for composure and courage during times of stress and that we may comfort those who are distraught.

Amen

Our Father we thank you for your gift
of this mortal life.

Help us each day to use this gift as you intended
it to be used.

We thank you for your gift of life eternal.
Help us to accept his greatest gift with Thanksgiving.

Amen

Our Father we pray not for ourselves
but for the proper use of ourselves.
We pray for enthusiasm for all of life,
that we may share our joy with others.

We pray for a faith so strong that we may
inspire others to be faithful and we pray
for the ability to love that we may help love
to spread throughout the world.

Amen

Our Father help us each day to treat our families and those dearest to us with patience and love.

Help us each day to be considerate and kind to those with whom we work and play.

And help us each day to encourage our friend to feel better about themselves.

This we ask in Christ's name.

Amen

Our Father help us pray to strive
for Christ centered life—not self centered.

To greet each day with enthusiasm, not with
fear.

To contribute to the welfare of our fellow man,
not to seek only personal gain.

To seek a moral life styled on self-discipline
not indulgence.

Amen

Our Father help us each day . . .

1. To combat weariness with enthusiasm

2. Difficulties with hard work

3. Frustration with patience

4. Jealousy with love

5. Despair with faith

6. Doubt with prayer

Your strength is our need and gift!
For this we thank you.

Amen

Our Father we thank you for the gift
of each new day. Help us to live life to its fullest,
knowing that tomorrow is not a reality—that
yesterday is gone—that today is the life we have.

Amen

If we only believe God has promised us life here and now, and life eternal.

Our promise to his to do justice, to love mercy, and to walk humbly with God. We know he will keep his promise.

Will we?

Amen

Our Father as we depart this class
help us in the coming week to take time to enjoy
and appreciate your works of beauty in nature,
and your works of beauty in man.

Amen

"Tree Study Brownstone"   M Cough '90

Our Father we ask for your healing hand
on the members of our class who are ill.

Help us to start each day of this week
with a prayer of thanksgiving on our lips
and a song in our hearts in honor
of your countless blessings.

Amen

Our Father in the new year
we pray you will help us to. . .

1. Be kinder than necessary
2. Speak gently
3. Listen attentively
4. Work joyously
5. Give generously
6. Serve cheerfully
7. Smile radiantly
8. Love unreservedly
9. Live victoriously

With you as our guide.
This we ask in your name.

Amen

Our Father we have enjoyed being a guest in your house this morning.

We invite you to be a guest in each of our homes during the coming week.

Amen

Our Father we ask for your healing hand
on the members of our class who are ill.

Guide us to start each day of this week
with a prayer of thanksgiving on our lips
and a song in our hearts in honor
of your countless blessings.

Amen

Our Father we thank you for this class and
for the message brought to us this day.

We pray you will inspire us to a life of service.
We pray for good health that we may use
our energy for composure and courage
during times of stress that we may comfort those
who are distraught.

Amen

Date 10/14/90

"LET YOUR LIGHT SO SHINE BEFORE
MEN THAT THEY MAY SEE YOUR
GOOD WORKS" AND GLORIFY YOUR
FATHER WHICH IS IN HEAVEN"!
OUR FATHER HELP US TO BE
YOUR TRUE SERVANTS IN A NEEDY
WORLD - MAY OUR MOTIVES BE
PURE AND OUR ACTIONS INSPIRED.
AMEN

Date 10/28/90

OUR FATHER WE THANK YOU FOR
THE EXCELLENT LESSON THAT WAS
BROUGHT TO US THIS MORNING. WE
PRAY YOU WILL BE WITH OUR TEACHERS
EACH SUNDAY. INSPIRE THEM TO
BE YOUR TRUE MESSENGERS. MAY
OUR MINDS AND HEARTS BE OPEN
TO RECEIVE AND HEAR THE WORDS
OF YOUR SERVANTS —
AMEN

117

Date __11/4/90__

DEAR GOD HELP US TO KNOW —
WHERE THERE IS DARKNESS THERE
CAN BE LIGHT, WHERE WEAKNESS —
STRANGTH, WHERE DASPAIR — HOPE
WHERE HATE — LOVE, WHERE DOUBT —
FAITH, AND WHERE DEATH — LIFE,
ALL THESE THINGS THROUGH
FAITH IN YOUR PROMISES —
                    AMEN

Date 1/11/90

DEAR GOD HELP US EACH DAY
TO ACCENTUATE THE POSITIVE -
TO STRIVE TO LIFT THE SPIRITS
OF OTHERS AND THEREBY OUR
OWN - TO LIVE WITH THE JOYOUS
KNOWLEDGE THAT WE ARE YOUR
CHILDREN, AND EACH DAY HAS
ITS PRECIOUS MEANING AND
OPPORTUNITY. HELP US TO LIVE
EACH DAY WITH YOU AS OUR
CONSTANT COMPANION -
                    AMEN

Date 11/18/90

OUR FATHER - PLEASE FILL OUR
HEARTS WITH LOVE SO THERE WILL
BE NO ROOM FOR HATE - FILL OUR
MINDS WITH GRATITUDE SO THERE
WILL BE NO ROOM FOR COMPLAINTS -
FILL OUR SOULS WITH JOY SO THERE
WILL BE NO ROOM FOR DEPRESSION -
MAY OUR FAITH BE SO STRONG
IT WILL CARRY US THROUGH ANY
STORM.
        AMEN

Date 11/25/90

OUR FATHER WE THANK YOU
FOR YOUR PROMISE TO HELP
US TURN FAILURES INTO SUCCESSES,
TEMPTATIONS INTO VICTORIES,
SELFISHNESS INTO SERVICE,
SORROWS INTO JOYS AND SIN
INTO SALVATION. THROUGH IT
ALL MAY OUR HEARTS AND MINDS
BE FOCUSED ON YOU!
AMEN

125

Date 11/18/90

OUR FATHER — PLEASE FILL OUR
HEARTS WITH LOVE SO THERE WILL
BE NO ROOM FOR HATE — FILL OUR
MINDS WITH GRATITUDE SO THERE
WILL BE NO ROOM FOR COMPLAINTS —
FILL OUR SOULS WITH JOY SO THERE
WILL BE NO ROOM FOR DEPRESSION —
MAY OUR FAITH BE SO STRONG
IT WILL CARRY US THROUGH ANY
STORM.
                    AMEN

Date 11/18/90

OUR FATHER — PLEASE FILL OUR
HEARTS WITH LOVE SO THERE WILL
BE NO ROOM FOR HATE — FILL OUR
MINDS WITH GRATITUDE SO THERE
WILL BE NO ROOM FOR COMPLAINTS —
FILL OUR SOULS WITH JOY SO THERE
WILL BE NO ROOM FOR DEPRESSION —
MAY OUR FAITH BE SO STRONG
IT WILL CARRY US THROUGH ANY
STORM.
                AMEN

Date 11/25/90

OUR FATHER WE THANK YOU
FOR YOUR PROMISE TO HELP
US TURN FAILURES INTO SUCCESSES,
TEMPTATIONS INTO VICTORIES,
SELFISHNESS INTO SERVICE,
SORROWS INTO JOYS AND SIN
INTO SALVATION. THROUGH IT
ALL MAY OUR HEARTS AND MINDS
BE FOCUSED ON YOU!
Amen

Date 12/2/90

OUR FATHER - HELP US WE
PRAY - TO USE OUR EARS TO
HEAR YOUR WORD - OUR EYES TO
READ YOUR WORD - OUR MINDS
TO UNDERSTAND YOUR WORD -
OUR WILLS TO OBEY YOUR WORD -
AND OUR FAITH TO ACTIVATE
YOUR WORD -

          AMEN

Date 12/9/90

OUR FATHER WE PRAY YOU WILL
GRANT US COURAGE IN TIMES
OF STRIFE — CHARACTER IN TIMES
OF TEMPTATION — COMPOSURE IN
TIMES OF CHAOS — EMPATHY
FOR THOSE IN NEED — ENTHUSIASM
FOR ALL OF LIFE AND FAITH
IN THE ULTIMATE VICTORY —
AMEN

135

Date 12/16/90

OUR FATHER MAY WE LEAVE
NOW WITH A RENEWED SPIRIT
SO WHAT WE SAY - WHAT WE DO
AND WHAT WE FEEL - WILL
REFLECT A KEENER SENSE OF
YOUR PRESENCE IN OUR LIVES.
AMEN

137

Date 12/23/90

OUR FATHER — MAY WE HAVE
THE TRUE SPIRIT OF CHRISTMAS
IN OUR MINDS AND IN OUR
HEARTS SO WE CAN WITH DEEP
REVERANCE, SAY THANK YOU FOR
THIS SUPREME GIFT — YOUR SON
JESUS CHRIST. MAY OUR LIVES
REFLECT OUR ACCEPTANCE OF
THIS GIFT —

Amen

139

Date 12/30/90

OUR FATHER WE THANK YOU
FOR THE YEAR PAST AND THE
YEAR TO COME — INSPIRE US TO
MAKE A NEW RESOLUTION EVERY
DAY — SO THAT EACH TODAY WILL
BE BETTER THAN YESTERDAY AND
EACH TOMORROW BETTER THAN TODAY
Ann

Your Own Prayers

Date _____

Date _____

Date _____

Date _____

Date _____

Date _____

Date _____

Date _____

Date _____

Date _____

Back Cover
*The First Presbyterian Church,
Greensboro, North Carolina*

by Molly Davis